POST CLASSIC

in memory of Moshe Nemeth (1923-2017)

ROOF BOOKS
NEW YORK

CONTENTS

an (in)vocation

sing to me emotionless exercise
tweet the essence of how i hear you
say "circumferential" "birthplace"

"infrastructure" "subway" dogma
say i hear you verbatim so sing
to me of intermissions and water

mark my name a logo pregnant
with handshakes sing to me of
material troops of fortified islands

harbor me eccentric i can't wait
to walk all these grounds fuck all
these canons their song a lone

stork an act of trying to use
ballet as frame to dramatize
certain collisions open wary

monumental battery sing to me
of mandates and public cruises
corporate contest high character
sample brass militant floor plan
in another war go by "the tower"
i like to think i grew up

on the ferry a history sold off
deliberately dance the dance of
evacuation party of anyone

else's torso not a head not
a snake not a woodpecker not
another story of residue and revelation

of chameleons their gavels sing to me
o competitive pitch o instrument
dissident supra horn desire generally

nothing is neutral so choreograph
and leave me food truck professional
drag interchangeable with muzzle

sing to me o pre-suppositional gloss
a non-public preview warehouse
to house the roles to play to get

used to sharing tourist injury
lifejacket adages a big ass umbrella
sing to me o institutional hashtag

chasm demolition accommodation
guarding guards sing to me o forms
of reservoir of retrospective fragility

statistics symbolic i dreamed
last night there was this weasel
i never use "beauty" for revenue

I

"...Perhaps this time she wouldn't call herself Helen; perhaps instead there might be recovered some sense of what mind was like before Homer, before the world went haywire & women were denied participation in the design & making of it. Perhaps someone might discover that original mind inside herself right now, in these times. Anyone might."

Alice Notley, "Homer's Art"

POST CLASSIC

to call myself natural consequence
to say "i shall not eat unless confused"

but again i'm in her voice, the original
fail the gauge set the covering

of even hands and feet it's this mouth
where shame holds origin where

female bodied fail where auto-
dysmorphic online shop therapy

can't cover the way i sing anti-
tongue shuffle boots cross campus

as if impossible to remember how she
walks the original body is not shameful

female fake i'm tired of scars
of explaining the use-value of fishnets

and leave you with this image as i exit
the mouth of eve and return to propaganda

to remember the milton who no longer
aims to defy death and time and chance

the so-called obvious choices as part
of a body rebelled dispelled to cheat

any angel who offers to stand
against the veined trunk of the apple

tree with target to marry branch
with breath with breast   channel

through gender reputation sacred
pocket watch   enshrined by history

there's a lot of tension in generic
theology where parallax snaps

she to i can't salvage control or
indoctrination it's unjust to try to wear

a body as seen through dashboard
insignificant in stereo call out

in defense of our esoteric union
new girls rise in every side

if leaving the garden is akin
to being struck by lightning

if the law is less abstract in
question marks less an empty

cavern than uncertain chronology
where every reptile loves

in tendencies if eve our singular
disciple if i learn to be less

annoyed in magical thinking
if i can become more we
become more simple reconciliation
with the word "holy" or "charisma"

or "debt" or "lonely" or "atone"

how speech might help
loss how our doubts seem

richer how code shifting
should not be severe

how there's always a way
to connect to how glaciers

are more than a giant hunk
of ice how articulate how we're all

intrinsically valuable how
operational how rigorous

how "magnetic" "counterfeit"
depersonalized home-making

how am i still driving in
the midst of so many inches

of hypothetical snow

how we get news changes how we fall
from memory collective how a person

becomes position(ed) how we forget
what it means to look telescopic to

say "no" how it's conducive to how
i want just possibility just crafted just

right how i worry we're not enough
producer just because sometimes

bearing present just isn't enough

i don't want death
hero of this epic

don't want to see
violence as the only

moment to talk about
how an empiricist feels

about definitions of virtue
of what we see only via

flights of birds or faith
or all these landscapes

i never paint because there's
always judgment always men

their conversations a ship
no one labels corrupt

slaughter begets daughter
begets institutional lip reading

please notice the amount
of ornamentation in temptation

of man turmoil takes various human
limbs connect them a game of if

what in this expansion optional
story starts in traditional structure

like backlit photograph farming for
the idea of farming and fixating

on things only a cardinal should see
our ships corrupt   what if we don't

fly don't float draw plain houses
with multiple trees   hear language

then feel something as if curtain
my costume   i just can't

fuck all this need to make
legible geysers of familiar

masochism   picnic table
elegance gone viral because

this time i write as fallen man
fallen from sermonizing miss-

understanding fallen it's
exceptional how often i want

entropy instead of haloes
or the sting supposed to

move you make you feel
marvel at responsibility

a beautiful indulgence where
i live by default exude a need

to wrangle institutional gods
by means of contracts i quote

here for security "only
victims tell stories in public"

most moments don't merit
big paper acting or the threat

of playing outside usual crutch
routine where i can't wait to

pretend to clear sidewalk for
the stench of available things

tailoring flavors my visual
hatred of mythical categories

shop talk photosynthesis
take design in a prompt who

can't metabolize drinks exotic
pawn shop we're all creatures

we take ourselves seriously
pretend i got privilege to pursue

one calling to pull down
my handlebars visit some

transitional shell when news
comes my rage sings of physical

priorities of distance support and
ancestral bookkeeping so this

great oration of comings compound
in a building i never notice

enthusiasms indulgence endemic
taxidermied floor plan hashtag

things to think about fully active
in mutual indifference i fail you see

dear e:

it's easy to tell a good story. it's easy to imagine beginnings, endings, and always the judgement of eve. it's easy to see oneself as narrator it's easy to proclaim something without question. what does it mean. to open one's eyes to see another man attack another man injuries involve blood suddenly because remember this is dramatic. a first vision of death. the killing of one's brother. how does one see after that?

to be responsible exhausting. to be labeled "historical figure," a visible articulation of confusion of outcomes so real and heartless and. it's exhausting to find yet another. wild man. a woman. tablet monstrous. who can count this reverie. of bullfrogs and cockroaches born covered. in fur. parents not proud. she part ape. a larger mythology. rationale for prostitution. i don't claim to take space in any feminist camp governance journey pronounced.

POST CLASSIC

in the beginning i introduce myself.
in the beginning i'm hoarse not fallen.
shame takes positive costume adorned
in glass limbs. in the beginning i hear
language lift the curtain. shift present tense
to back stage. in the beginning we all become
something. no question of heroism. no
imaginary tables to set. outcome comes
real because it's heartless to only touch
in and promise. like the surprise of a required
dressing room mandate to introduce
myself by identity marker i'm not one.
who makes excuses for any kind of omen.
or hears tales on front lawn. if you heed me
i will devour "him" supplant any graces with
statutes of matriarchy. her simple contours.
troublesome branches. sing to me
of consort and reparation. in the beginning
non-belonging attempt to wear video
camera enabled skin. gene change anomaly
renal enrapture. live transitional cell hard
to see. non-invasive conversation. i take on
personas. a man who won't speak. won't

reflect on what it means to block traffic. keep

fingers crossed. align empty ritual with

devout headshake. gather typical clientele.

cannon littered with bodies. a building i

don't notice. in the beginning that sting.

see so much destruction it helps me

understand my own tomb structure

identity portrait where railroad tracks

undeniable watchtower effigy tell me

take more than a cast of my hand

exile epic latex reliquary ephemera nylon

bygone i don't know how to greet this

subject suppose welcomeis formula

reasonably complicated   memorial

industrial complex   imagine this body

and override it infectious mannequin

undesirable actor   paid norming enzyme

active fever society   bayonet names

unstitch you so intestines fall out we keep

running away from   harvest scorch

of every name i make in order to learn

this language   defensive vagabond private

misfortune   underline only the important

activity of offering   screen test carnivore

faux relic of private behavior conjurer

of housewife morning ritual retro

catacomb   i'm aware and vocal deem

usual body hassle harlot impersonator

resist authentic skill   virulent skull

coat of triple letters   formal suggestions

for prototype   i love a good gallery

cry   walk a mile   without completing

the circuit   an actual character   pre-

implantation asthmatic decorum sneak

important meteorpathetic glance take this

definition of contact hour keratin savvy

final chapter write : someone survives

POST CLASSIC

i become emotional only where i can see
the path of the samurai instead of photos

don't want   to replicate the experience
of being summarized   repackaged

for a world where spelling counts   and
cultivate is a positive word   my snake

is not quite   between the apples yet
i build an excuse for expressivismintuit

different ways to explicate weakness in
prototype   my own story   feudal sworn

jackets   sanctuary synthetic assembly
i want every joint customizable   credentialed

auto-immunocentric   still life with remote
control unabashedly artificial   a long

way from superimposed device schedule
stand-in dummy oracle   i walk a mile

want to rot in these shoes   then design
my own calf muscle knee cap ligament

exist   in movement   move

opposite   elevation   takes arm

at slide physician   girdle it

soldier wax anatomic   good

manner gun lesson   half

court hair cut please   i was

as a people who weapon ritual

seating don't know   circular

knife toss   way to get   here   together

tunic   as fodder   as warming

as fame exhibition   shoulder

posture up my friend   coffee

house me   reckless exaggerated

hot mess   fictive maker   common

passive vandalism   ready to be

found a skeletontravels counter

bullet   counter public   event

invitational like   conformity

emblem   historic gruff   starched

my story begins laden   with models

clerical supernatural   obedient

bibliographic questions   of plural

mountains   momentary contest

enough led   i need place need

one-page proposal   sell-weaning

hyper-grammatic intent tower

photo shower   one-man future

curatorial disbelief   microwaveable

hello   manological   peep show

II

"Tell me about a complicated man.
Muse, tell me how he wandered and was lost
When he had wrecked the holy town of Troy..."

The Odyssey, Book One
trans. Wilson

"Sing to me of the Man, Muse, the man of twists and
          turns
driven time and again off course, once he had
          plundered the hallowed heights of Troy."

The Odyssey, Book One
trans. Fagles

POST CLASSIC
for David Buuck

don't worry you'll realize
it's monotheism
that causes all problems

it's the expletives
in mainstream parchment
marriage between blood

agriculture and the key
to the armoire already
constitutes informed

consent the strategy
du jour for functioning
outlet sales think

of elbowing as code
for morality a mass
in my neck another

indicator of the benign
neglect too profound
to be bitter too neurotic

in the face of "regular"
experience a common
test for the intangible

exodus or the devouring
that takes place when no one
knows the difference

between tv preachers and
the fanatic's empathy fully
planned prepared to play

hopeful to grab the snake
by the entrails and offer up
a macro view of creation

POST CLASSIC

a heron is not
the kind of bird
to wear such
a hollow dug
out to conduct
dust public i
breathe get
heirless imagine
her distant from
all biography

of course we have wings
disrupt history aren't
designed to crash where
curriculum finds
any term to serve
comment box resistance
here's a different voice
threaded with frustration
a force all her own
dividing legitimacy into

a pelican can't
hold us she performs
listening out loud
pregnant with ways
of marking intervals
an act of borrowing
monotony cocktail
take notice her
self-bounding narrative
with respect and pliance

write about the bird
cage they say write about
blood transfusion gum
surgery anger volume gout
in this harem we're
flightless decorative
chicks husband least
concern husband as if
a kind of literacy
network physical visualize
the house the dog the car

look to an infographic to
escape anxiety each entrance
risks to be a scene for
interpretation relevantly
hazy like any memory
of crossing the Outerbridge
in an effort to inhale logos
in an effort to figure out
water travel punctuation
breech any exchange   we

know my protagonist she's becoming
idiomatic an only character afraid
to bring emotion back capsized
in ghostwriter quarantined wealth
trashy she's becoming someone who uses
the word "engage" a lot instead of
sheriff dope dick   bandana gore
lantern out   come out admit mirth
and other weaker areas predictably lady-
like predictably affable this new day

it's where i locate gesture a complete
molt signifies superiority a new bill
self-accessible in theory   at best
an excerpt of how it feels to be spit
on euphemism for familiarity cast as
lines   who show circumstance
in plaster who fly in every direction at will
perch only when suspect i become what
i know outside of questions of happiness
pill pajamas staph temporary teeth real hair

for the bureaucracy give no
empowerment objects are glass
made a formality cat or no cat
still i learn to lift the mouse
to think of the floor as grass i like
to avoid fostering generic stability

remember when we used to go
to the movies & feel young & cry in
the primary care physician's office i live
in the country gotta get a new bag

well oxygen is a step forward
to dream i guess we wear t-shirts
matching is a kind of satisfaction
there are rules for that we don't
follow there are wine bars for that
i know how to zeitgeist hypothetical
monosyllabic in sandals in self-care
i know all about first words like zebra
garbage aggression imbibe the nuance
of new kicks an epigraph to process

PROEM

dear epic   let's look back
to canvas   return gesture
as primal part of the earliest
genre of parlor games balderdash
garden of continuous charade
outside of the history of history
we don't engage don't flaunt
homecoming obscure rhetoric

border progression repurpose family
prayer sing to me of use   tell
me a story of practice air conditioning
gutter fancy sing to me again because
there is no new error no prophecy
of dancing violation let's begin in request

POST CLASSIC

if i say we have postcards to send
if i say please worship pages
tattoos of our beliefs order

season order commerce
welcome interpretation general
fashion statement active knowledge

if i say i was born statuesque
only in my demeanor who promises
everyone who promises to repent

historical sequence continues
to hurt and hurt and it's not easy
to deal scientifically with feelings

individual limbs and parts of the body
the crocodile still life among us
present day archaeology parts of

the body no shame our word
for everyone who promised
a city is thus always

possible always community

cheated creditor methods

breathing methods inert

remember a story is just

another kind of constraint

i want to travel through

pleasure in use is just a sign

of just creation and yet i don't

want to cultivate "the plan" give

advice through law i'm no

different inside our condition

romper friendly jukebox brogue

it can be said   harm

is easy to see   if i fall

in love with my own

anagram admit to being confused

when i feel like a painting full

of bodies wholly scaled

where desperate i want

mastery laser tag a feeling

of being accountable

for every assumption

even rodents accomplish

if i say guilt
is one of the biggest
flaws of our
civilization because

we always have both
feet on some battlefield

analog like robots
who vote for all

the wrong voices
deliberate in deliverance

goat framed photographer
of unruly bodies unruly

because i don't align
referential because i wear

my anatomy like
a dance card
if i exercise daily
my lipstick prerogative

if i come to terms

with a prefix like free

if i pretend to understand

how to label my body

in all its gender resent

playoff fever if my hands

were just a tiny bit bigger

i would palm a basketball

and grow a few more streets

dear e:

where is the basic question, sum of each suspect now amplified. it's hard to isolate my objectives, hang them on a dress form informed by proximity. if i can take a hunk of styrofoam and cloak it in my clothes then pretend to name her hallmark of heterosexuality.

i lack the proficiency to be real in my reading of images and high tops. i feel slayed by emotion more often than my gut permits me admit.

what i need to believe is that i won't die gay and alone in the woods covered in ticks.

what i need to believe is inaccurate geometry. doppler shift perhaps we're all the same crude protein game.

POST CLASSIC: [DE]PART

don't know how

to move away i

only want to be

in this public

date specific condo

migraine rental thug

try to entertain me

sense of initiation

promise hurdles navigate

rights remember only

i see problem

geography apologetic this

episode takes face

phobic cymbal tattoo

each ankle solar-

powered my turtle

guide moment to

sapphic emo sewage

fixate on relocation

process seaward steward

potential harm derelict

scuttle deck i

don't know physical

lease lingo walkout

monologue as way

of validation all

these threads coarse

i don't notice my own

forays in expression

refer to self

post productive post

composed wager my

medium here lead

discussion it's more

important to be

haphazard than gifted

III

"Today's 'memory boom' reflects less an abandonment of history than a cultural shift toward public feeling as a source of knowledge."

Erika Doss, from *Memorial Mania*

POST CLASSIC: ACCOUNT

o the shapes economy
makes out of the same
old garden sewn
with bad seeds empty

plot in place of head-
stone overgrown water-
soaked pebbles i reach
recount what an arm

we had labor-posed tech-
toned swallows keys
figurative sun stroke
chin pierce jaw shrug

again call attention to
marks the act names them
"pretext for anticipation"
my own days etch auto

martyr here lies a classic
survivor renegade sailor
potential bird metaphor
promise for counting place

the body so we leave
absolve bar stool choreography
python tablet lapse argot
cliché i'm tired of reading

journeys & women memorized
soil food trucks the body is not
a text not hard not tempted
deviant common flood binary

photoshoot checklist can't
confect lesbian look haute
dickies trend to obsessional
work boot commodity

"you never see" the guide
tells me somewhere still
there i return   learn to
wake up suspended finesse

exaggerate big trucks
hair twin pac manic hemo-
globin whiskey bitch
textbook holy last minute

this body is a cave
because it's easier
to be abstract
than mourning

POST CLASSIC

any hydrant trumps a sunset's duties i feel

injured skunk trots my gait rings agility ring

exit this office carriage liver spot life coach

confident   sin begets sin begets sin begets

vehicle horse dawn tap dancer basically i

just want to run stubborn   underscore

the common urge to praise a natural follower

of hard exercise and biblical shoveling

i dream in hiatus   wear warnings dormant

rabid   i'm attracted to hydrophobia

and crawl spaces vast in ascent discharge

ecosystemic   thunder suit solstice

where would i be without image banked

& now when you
ask for a souvenir
that is natural
i dig deep to afford

antiquity high tide
palm trees date back
to before ceramic coasters
before the idea of

unrequited became an empty
bench on the edge of every
road hover crane-style tractor
antsy i feel you on summer

vacation all agency full
of recyclable cans who
the enemies are less
apparent in the road

squatting amidst seashells
flags miscellaneous towers
what checkpoint say
i can't   imagine

part of the problem with eggnog is artificial observance

i believe in feeling and binding and bonding and

bondage there's no blanket for the conversion

process where pirates fuck machines but redact

intimacy with locking jaws myth softer exchanges

i don't like to show my teeth or nail polish

or collection of paper dolls and poodle stickers

if "get out of jail free" cards are symptomatic

of tycoon escapee skyrockets then i want

to be replaced by a unicycle committed

to the beauty of an ordinary wheel a bully

breed of simple cavorting it might feel easier

to be comfortable figure skating please carry the

torch   we can only be convicted for expression

never dream about deserts

will my quasi rest to rely on greenery

as if my own fig tree could happen

as if no market too close

but now i resist brick

acknowledge someone disposes

of every note in the wall

find my one space of habit

a tourist sculpture mass prayer

trance i can't help but touch

shoulders stowed i can't help

but turn away primitive marriage

& so i learn to filter my water & my breath my manic

trigger fawning more than intercept destroy toy

car phonic components & allow myself to feel angry

in fact irate with every rocket every fertilizer every

nozzle point evaluation phase redeployment ponzi pillar iron

drone advance fraud & who photographs them casual

arrow system currency troubles like when i choose

between my own or a collective voice to build a political house

worth living worth noticing the difference

between tunnel & residential life conversations are

most valuable when questing after attitudes or dogs

call myself honest if   & only in routine

POST CLASSIC: AGAIN

compromise without reason inert impetus to ground backstory in wanderings in the iron chef edition of public failure but you can't see the basket i can't help internal search formal garb complex present i feel pretty tough all driverless cycle night bridge theme advanced election jockey have a seat feel let down in opponent town baby you don't want to answer these emails dispute famed fantasy court asynchronous i got my avalanche on surrogate apostle know what's known self-created chronologically logographic i'm so not relational

POST CLASSIC
for Anselm Berrigan

this is a manmade pond populated by tadpole

imports to support a need to be visibly

expensive overlook who's frog-like expansive

we grow up to be we who cling to thread-

bare steel lattice i rely here on memory

instead of imagination because no one believes

desire in sudden necessity of wading on a walk

across tick-laden fields   step gently in

inevitable mud it isn't insects who betray

me who sing of infancy in statue form

this one example of many landmarks marked

precisely for data a physical birdcage

marmot governing Cropsey even the wayback

machine deems scarlet the robin who approach

i don't stand outside anymore can't stand

all flowers in frequent display trope of visible

breathing meme-able yet again the question

of money of exertion of stripling storied

historical cell ordinary habit model of it

isn't landmark to call millipedes fancy

POST INADEQUATE

the fact of becoming necessary

to want in   build a way

essential quality performance of

a material thing like to draft a paper

is to write until we exhaust ourselves

but never the idea of exhaustion image

falling short in attainment might be positive

because the idea is to fail safe take what

feels like danger   thwart it we need

miss-adventure to remember why default

looks valuable why our hero is never

just a person or visible ankle sprain

to decline in strength the fact
of bankruptcy variously confused
with sense of person success
obsolete without slight fault
the story clears its connotations
small gasp association with movies
i miss chat again a sequence
of geography or what's important
this is the narrative i tell myself
to revise beauty operatic compact
cover remember lipstick regulation
pin up decals substantively counter
"poor health" a positive impulse
like proverbial nails appreciate
broken machinery and not easy
answers my sequester defense true
but never interesting because it isn't
wanting defective electrical miss-leading

what is social? what apology? what mouth-
piece impious subjective lateral doubt
other words for "i have feeling(s)" common
miss-translation deems "security" only halfway
a journey functions as voiceover for confusion
& scripture & survival almost monologue
in purpose approached parallel to drama
"great men" part with war falter over
idiom not all dictionaries mark each page
for interruption not all armies gather boredom
as a bank of old words to turn to because
without divisiveness a chorus only comments   .
on acts of everyday   dear epic why can't
ghosts talk about disgust and desire reborn
why tigers   mown grass   heroic monsters
husband every intention what   is control

IV

You strive ceaselessly, what do you gain?
[...]
Do we build a house forever?
Do we make a home forever?

The Epic of Gilgamesh,
Tablet X, trans. Foster

POST CLASSIC

a riverboat is one way to promise
to get air circulating like questions

of hierarchy rectify & perhaps process
ballet as invention simple local

movement   be my horse ask to be
told a story swollen with hallow magic

a hats off narrative mandate to perform
earnestness as choice where boundaries

are called anniversary or vocation
& a woman walking more precious stone

i want to hear you in differentiation

when i say i'm driving through

mountains i mean not just filth

skepticism pronoun   staccato is

ordinary reception like rabies or

powerpoint or generic welcoming verbs

redemption is fascinating   a narrator

with personality   my hero dissolves

all men build fences instead of hauntings

she draws on emotion & other vocabularies

of management somehow located

between two houses yet outside of any

home underground roofless still hosting

directives are always fully preposterous
to begin focus on lyric as weighty speech

weighted because no period costume serves
rapture proxy for roughness for posture

annotated a heat map need to see
precision   sincerely its outlets public

intimacy laden social   each limb
should concern us each visage perhaps

constructive our rapport steers
imitation severs anatomy from

i know i respect common sense worry
about desirable & human & ecology &

anger but no one asks us   a hypothesis
defines discrete dysfunction & providence

to say i don't read the newspaper is miss-leading
the problem isn't offense it's where to put the ball

how to reconcile   the past is important
because i need to understand how to shoot

from another's shoes say "be mindful of the air
you inhabit" take up require imagine a construction

who holds up a mirror works as autograph book
& cliff-side bleacher seats   my bed

is uncomfortable where sense reckons splinters
i'm adulting so hard activity theory perspective

say to this project i have feelings like anger
and drama neither portable sanctuary

psychometrically viable visible i speak only
with strangers tell them i'm interested in names

not characters a weird notion of public exclusion
of indistinct shouting   carry into monolith

after the descent i stitch together blood
type in favor of showmanship a cappella
multifaceted in our conversion narrative

driven by tablets and injury and various
drugs dug up to replace boundless anatomy
aim to earn rumor shrouded in shipwreck

temptation historically iron more powerful
than prophecy and other currency excessive
i become transfuse by how enthusiasm

wears the weight of detail how meaningful
is defined randomly a substitute for authentic
connection rather a bandage parasitic

lab coat lap dog sterile lyric epistolary
gestational play de facto rehabilitation clan
stranger i ask after the defense commercial

after ants gather to assert behavioral vice
in flip chart desert process let's not boast
or bench service plot neuroplasticity

equipment commission i say sustain
me enabling matrices inventive most
mornings a tree is just a tree

POST CLASSIC

there's no reason to smell without
fire ask after steel wool skin fracture
karaoke cds
        how many live on landing
strip stairmaster table tennis bloodbath
portrait of more barrels and hay and
outlet malls ambidextrous in bad
timing bridge layer
        say things just to be
nasty fiesta ware desire to beat
mannequin games crochet hook
empathy
        i recuse myself scourge
of dirt island activity theory gadfly
do the adolescent dance pre-
requisite for potential wound empire
accent over my historical self
        say dissent is easy
in the subjunctive as my character
evolves   value accountable talk

dear e:

let's talk about processes rely on stories of contradiction by way of stacking images but how do we understand a name increasingly fallen like "you are wonderful" or self-evident democracy

let's talk about empathy self-exiled, it's how i try to find meaning this week, how i respond where appropriation causes harm, random intention has intention perhaps designed to

document historiography one of many relationships to listen to then listen back emotionless like commemorative culture like any exercise of man building man long after

the event untenable a signature riff on memorialization or public feeling let's talk about a sequence of geography push back on losing yourself in lineage in regime change real estate

class variegated to emit what happens at every cemetery let's say i'm *not* out there alone climbing some stupid mountain happy to pop off and practice facility in damage let's say

this is victory this is war this is protest fatigue a brief gestural eulogy for appropriate moments for in-depth tourism danger-zone connectivity let's mingle with monument

counter constructivism say "in the trenches" my temporary mode of mourning my sensitized education needs no friends

POST PEDAGOGY

i got a deep problem
with evaluation. there's
a method to glancing

over our hypothetical
futures—it ain't standard.
effective needs improvement.

who wants to live
on a disgusting iceberg
accredited? who wants

to become harbor-
reliant treeless bodies?
migratory swallows

rockhop from finding
to findings like cloud-
based floral arrangements

or failed cell small
balloons. i'm always taking
a look at our project

plan always trying to use god
in the pejorative. i'm interested
in indirect perception

as countrywide deployment
sort of a pantomime of nature
of gettin' aligned along

our improvement journey
all about still lives and stilling
lyric responsibilities. i'm not

a woman. lack proper
rubric etiquette outcome
verb funerals are powerful

like google and importing
forms as dude hat
patterns for shooting

guards. i'm also hard
to find in hotel room
casting couch tableaus.

catalytic pocket squares
convey empathy no head-
stone can shout out

to legacy to litany to
sibling rosters complete.
dissent is not exclusion

but a duty to construct
myself then kill off
professional martyr

pregnant with tactile
definitions of intermission
and balance and i don't

want to make things easy
take an oath or vouch for
affectation as its own

warning i always want
recorded images ingestible
capsules a way to get

misty moved to my core.
what can be gained only
through a close reading

machine close to combat
communication diagnostics.
really i just want to neighbor

sincerely valorize the unstable
stand behind knights in training.
i can't share ladies i love

POST CLASSIC

in order to have authentic relationships each line
item must display its own ligament personality

in order to compete on the court of mansplainery
this body must learn to dissolve into itself not

as concession to poor architecture but rather
in quasi celebration of chaos of the whirlpool

in order to think back to my own autobiography
where i never was small forward never reincarnation

of worthy never sacred never dynasty big game
farmer who harvests machinery instead of indigo,

livestock, or administrators in order to live with
carnage without becoming basic product sage revel

i take on wild man accretion wear body hair like
let's wade through that muddy water playoff field

of enjoyable grooming well-documented social vertebrate
dream of cease fire & inner tubes & free freestyle lessons

finally unpacking my own archive of contestable passports
& genetic shame mongering there's a reason i wore a cape

all these pictures & you think & you see me & really it's
just another girl wearing a little red riding hood costume

or a boy with a hot rod case i only want to expand
access to things like physical comedy pinky rings or

finding myself stuck in the limo i never thought i'd ride
all the mistranslations of i want to be attached & all that to

more than syllables women & game or an evidence first kind
of essay on carbon dating conventional spacing is it wrong

to want to toss my gauntlet again & again & find some big
gay old-fashioned skate park where this is a private freewrite

endemic to my body can't be a lie because these essays can't
become undone again austere quarters call me snow globe

stand in lovable failure what questions become systematic
become subjecting become subject for it's strange to see

in inverse like tracking the divine name to find her un-enrolled
carrying seeds of a co-pilot of a narrative who came out

mimesis constellation candid in my reading of desire
as only physical a giant stuffed animal poised

in public lens longing for a regular family crest to model
myself after because every garden is gone i grew up outside

of nature of courtship of seasons who change me i wear
my tongue like a stuffed mammal with ears detachable you

can't ask me to eliminate any one sense in order to prove
vitality or exceptionalism or at least draft a few new angles

through which to find a dismantling of the shoes we bring
as reminder to notice the level of ornamentation i notice

my own visual routine my deep hatred for skit acting
& the omnipresent threat of playing in any troubled

POST CLASSIC

sing to me of parachutes. impose luxury
measures, active farming, ceasefire mural
sourced from quicksand & argument morale

sing to me so i know what's admissible,
a foundation of wonder instead
of inflammatory markets, where you

are your body of water polluting
& i am lost again born throughout
year of the dragon   sing to me

of accuracy and empathy of health
first attitudinal shifts of systemic intolerance
of exertion of using the entire body

to be discouraged   sing to me of
immune systems unplugged, redact
mown evidence of post-endeavor

malaise brain fog ongoing disaster
sing to me of orthostasis of no shame
in redefining distance code shift

across consensus to the sirens who
sing only of history & i can't tell them
to listen to disease categorize imaginary

harm as ongoing matter   tickets
bought   ambivalence sleep   sing
to me gadfly bias definitively i depend

POSTSCRIPT

welcome to this fable
of our time of the banal
material that leads us
to the origin of every sin

this fable welcomes sin
because we believe that
civilization is falling
& the only text to share

a bad book not a fable
who cultivates clarity
like a job description
should not hinder

authenticity after surgery
my voice changed bathed
in original sin a metallic locus
who holds secret pork

& other memorabilia the epistle
a scary form of relationship
where affect circulates like
nightstand goldfish complimentary

dog walk haircuts my subject
believes in first gesture perspiration
checkpoint evacuation games
jealous of the men on postcards

& their use of umbrellas to reenact
privilege remember anti-memoir urgency
perhaps dissent is when spring comes
i don't care to name trees invite

what's legible out of iris comes hand
paint brush poor will on branch
whiskered puppet i hope to invoke
frailty as sting perhaps hidden

until i wade into the Mediterranean
read plastic as hurt picturesque
a response to guards in effigy
i choose the bird card arms devout

re-translation note

Paradise Regained, John Milton's "brief epic" and sequel to *Paradise Lost,* arguably revolves around the relationship between heroism and obedience. The poem begins:

> I who e're while the happy Garden sung,
> By one man's disobedience lost, now sing
> Recover'd Paradise to all mankind,
> By one man's firm obedience fully tri'd...

This is a very different vision of man from the start of *Paradise Lost:* "Of Man's First Disobedience, and the Fruit/Of that Forbidden Tree." If it is disobedience, in the form of Eve's agency, that leads to the fall (however debatably fortunate), then is obedience a hallmark of postlapsarian time?

POST CLASSIC began with this question of "obedience" in mind. It struck me that neither the *Odyssey* nor *Gilgamesh* are obedient texts—and their disobedience is grounded in female agency. Odysseus's wife, Penelope, subverts any typical marriage plot by spending her nights unraveling the shroud she weaves by day. She refuses suitors, insisting they wait until she completes the project she never intends to finish.

In *Gilgamesh,* we meet two immortal, independent "working women"—Shamhat, "the sacred prostitute," and Shiduri, "the tavern keeper." Shamhat's magic is what moves the plot of *Gilgamesh* forward—she domesticates Enkidu, civilizes "the wild man," and introduces him to Gilgamesh. Shamhat makes it possible for man to become man. Similarly, Shiduri speaks to a broken Gilgamesh honestly, "You will never find the eternal life/that you seek." This assertion is demonstrative of how Shiduri she refuses to entertain Gilgamesh's fear of death and frenzied mourning. King or no king, it is Shiduri who knows "the best way for a man to live."

What if, as Lisa Robertson asks in *Debbie: An Epic,* "narrative might annotate an ambivalence"? What if, instead of existing on the periphery, women are mythopoetic agents whose actions propel them from plot device to central to the "hero's journey"? i'm attracted to the *Odyssey* and *Gilgamesh* because of this trope of wayward women who undermine so called "heroic men."

**

INSTANT CLASSIC (Roof Books, 2013) aimed to investigate how a body becomes both censored and commodified, taking its cue from the publication history of *Paradise Lost*. When i began POST CLASSIC in the summer of 2013, my idea was to create a sequel to INSTANT CLASSIC, that worked through the earliest epics, with the central experiment being to see how a contemporary monomyth might function, full of conflicting translation(s), queerness and querying, and a commitment to subverting the way bodies read as female are expected to journey.

As with INSTANT CLASSIC, i began by creating word lists out of the books that called to the project—a range of translations of the *Odyssey* and *Gilgamesh*, lesbian pulp fiction "classics", and poetic and theoretical texts. My writing process is often procedural—i create word lists, decide on a specific form a poem will take, map out the way i hope to engage with the "narrative arc" of a canonical epic, and then create. The poems are meant to be both mine and not-mine. i work with words on an individual level, but i do not generate the words myself. i'm interested in the idea that language speaks differently when its normative use is disrupted—i.e. sitting down to "write" versus working through a predetermined set of language.

However, after finishing a draft of POST CLASSIC in the spring of 2016, i found myself unwilling to put the work into the world—in the throes of the 2016 Presidential Campaign i noticed my relationship to how i used language changing, fueled by a sense of urgency. In the fall of 2016, following a series of particularly egregious campaign speeches by Donald Trump, full of racist/sexist/homophobic/ableist rhetoric reminiscent of Nazism, i decided that POST CLASSIC needed to be entirely redone. The epic needed to come out of me and my own subject position. The hostility and unreliability of Trump's campaign rhetoric led me to believe that the current moment was not one in which i was comfortable sharing authorship or depending on other sources.

**

Stephen Mitchell introduces his approach to translating *Gilgamesh* as motivated by a desire to "find a genuine voice for the poem...to re-create the ancient epic, as a contemporary poem, in the parallel universe of the English language." Mitchell's approach to translating a text that exists in fragments, a narrative full of holes, is to acknowledge that to translate is to contemporize, to re-vision a text. In an interview with *Library Journal* (9/1/2017), writer/translator Daniel Mendelsohn discusses the myriad of translations of Homer's *Odyssey* in existence: "Homer's Greek famously has many aspects—it's archaic but also moves swiftly, it has nobility of tone but isn't stiff, it is highly stylized and formal but never seems artificial—and a great truth of Homer translations is that each translation tends to get one or two—but rarely all—of those facets." In her "Translator's Note", Emily Wilson writes, "All modern translations of ancient texts exist in a time, a place, and a language that are entirely alien from those of the original... Homer is, and is not, our contemporary" (87-8).

Reading these reflections on the act of translation led me to decide that i would need to re-translate *POST CLASSIC*. i'd thought of the initial draft of the poem its own kind of translation, an intervention into the worlds depicted in *Gilgamesh* and the *Odyssey*. So, my job then became deciding how to re-translate the text back into my own language, on and in my own terms, through a process that would involve active voice intervening on the text's content more than a homophonic or sound-based translation. Given that i'd begun the book several years earlier, and given the results of the 2016 presidential election, i wanted to think about the potential of "re-translation" as another kind of world-making.

In "Homer's Art", Alice Notley refers to the *Odyssey* and the *Iliad* as "public stories...stories for men about a male world". Anne Waldman describes her own epic impulse (in "Epic & Performance") as "I needed as twentieth-war-ravaged-century inhabitant-woman to take on male energy".

With Notley and Waldman echoing in my mind, i decided to approach my poem line by line; to shift its vocabulary from procedurally generated to subjectively organic. i wanted to try to revision the epic as story as it might be contemporarily told. i wanted to be accountable for the way i compose. i wanted to be disobedient because disobedience is generative, originary, central to any creation myth.

To offer a sense of where the poem itself began, select "source texts" are included as "allusions" here.

**

suppose when i use the word "epic" it becomes a narrative that's contemporary.

suppose there is no garden to begin with, to fall from, to weed. instead a place where disobedience is desired and desirable, alternative fact constitutes sin in this space.

suppose a *post classic* where "post" indicates a relationship to information, and "classic" signifies the familiar yet outstanding, the time-tested recipient of one's gaze.

welcome to this work of a certain age.

select allusions

Gilgamesh
    Trans. Stephen Mitchell (2006)
    Trans. Benjamin R. Foster (2002)
    Trans. N.K. Sandars (1960)
Homer, *The Odyssey*
    Trans. Emily Wilson (2018)
    Trans. Robert Fagles (2009)
    Trans. Stanley Lombardo (2000)
    Trans. Robert Fitzgerald (1998)
Nicholas Abraham and Maria Torok, *The Shell and the Kernel* (1994)
Sara Ahmed, *Living a Feminist Life* (2017)
Sara Ahmed, *On Being Included: Racism and Diversity in Institutional Life* (2012)
Anonymous, *Dyke Farm* (1964)
Kevin Bales, *Disposable People: New Slavery in the Global Economy* (2012)
Joseph Campbell, *The Hero with a Thousand Faces* (1949)
Kim Case, *Deconstructing Privilege* (2017)
Carol Clanton, *Gay Interlude* (1961)
Mihaly Csikszentmihalyi, *Creativity: Flow and the Psychology of Invention* (2013)
Ann Cvetkovich, *An Archive of Feelings: Trauma, Sexuality, and Lesbian Public Cultures* (2003)
Erika Doss, *Memorial Mania: Public Feeling in America* (2012)
Mickey Eliason, *The Dyke Diagnostic Manual* (2013)
Roderick Ferguson, *The Reorder of Things: The University and Its Pedagogies of Minority Difference* (2012)
Madeline Gins, *What the President Would Say and Do* (1984)
Marianne Hirsch, *The Generation of Postmemory: Writing and Visual Culture after the Holocaust* (2012)
Jill Johnston, *Lesbian Nation: The Feminist Solution* (1974)
Susana Kaiser, *Postmemories of Terror* (2005)
John Milton, *Paradise Regained* (1671)
Alice Notley, *Alma, or The Dead Women* (2006)
Alice Notley, *Certain Magical Acts* (2016)

Alice Notley, *Coming After: Essays on Poetry* (2005)

Alice Notley, *Disobedience* (2001)

Alice Notley, *Homer's Art* (1990)

Lisa Robertson, *Debbie: An Epic* (1997)

Ann Summerhill, *Debut of a Belated Lesbian* (1968)

Valerie Taylor, *The Girls in 3-B* (1959)

Valerie Taylor, *Stranger on Lesbos* (1960)

Valerie Taylor, *Return to Lesbos* (1963)

Tereska Torres, *Women's Barracks* (1950)

Michel-Rolph Trouillot, *Silencing the Past: Power and the Production of History* (1995)

Anne Waldman, *Gossamurmur* (2013)

Anne Waldman, *The Iovis Trilogy: Colors in the Mechanism of Concealment* (2011)

Anne Waldman, *Trickster Feminism* (2018)

Anne Waldman, *Vow to Poetry* (2001)

James E. Young, *The Texture of Memory: Holocaust Memorials and Meaning* (1994)

acknowledgments

Earlier versions of these poems have appeared in *The Brooklyn Rail, P-QUEUE, Supplement v. 1, The Recluse, Asterisk, Mantis,* and *Infiltration: An Anthology of Innovative Poetry from the Hudson River Valley.* Thank you to the editors and publishers of these texts.

"an (in)vocation" and "POST CLASSIC: AGAIN" were both written in collaboration and conversation with the artist Jon Allen.

"POST CLASSIC" ("a heron is not") is dedicated to the memory of Jerry Gafio Watts (1953-2015). Jerry always reminded me that I am first and foremost a poet.

Thank you to my colleagues and students at Bard College and the Institute for Writing & Thinking. I'm lucky to write alongside all of you. Many of these poems began with our work together.

This book is also indebted to Ammiel Alcalay, Joshua Beckman, Charles Bernstein, Anselm Berrigan, Brandon Brown, David Buuck, John Coletti, CAConrad, Nicole Eisenman, Al Filreis, Derek Furr, E. Tracy Grinnell, Wayne Koestenbaum, Matt Longabucco, Eileen Myles, Alice Notley, Phil Pardi, Andrea Quaid, Joan Retallack, Ariel Reznikoff, Judah Rubin, Frank Sherlock, Anne Waldman, Dana Ward, Simone White.

Finally, I owe many thanks to the support of my mom, dad, Rebecca, Dan, Bomber, Yogi, Maureen, and Lola.